Water Plants

All Wet!

by Ellen Lawrence

Consultant:

George Bowes, PhD
Professor Emeritus
Department of Biology
University of Florida
Gainesville, Florida

BEARPORT
PUBLISHING

New York, New York

Credits
Cover, © Jelger Herden/Minden Pictures/FLPA and © Yuriy Kulik/Shutterstock; 2, © tea maeklong/Shutterstock; 2–3, © Videowokart/Shutterstock; 3TL, © joloei/Shutterstock; 3BR, © Chaowalit Seeneha/Shutterstock; 4, © Svetlana Foote/Shutterstock; 4–5, © Yuriy Kulik/Shutterstock; 6, © Frans Lanting/FLPA; 7, © blickwinkel/Alamy; 8T, © subin pumsom/Shutterstock; 8B, © Luciano Candisani/Minden Pictures/FLPA; 9, © Willem Kolvoort/Nature Picture Library; 10T, © Asmus/Shutterstock; 10B, © Christian Fischer; 11, © dpa picture alliance/Alamy; 11L, © ImageBroker/FLPA; 12, © apomares/IstockPhoto; 13, © Vilainecrevette/Shutterstock; 14, © WaterFrame/Alamy; 15, © vkilikov/Shutterstock; 16T, © Steve Trewhella/FLPA; 16B, © Norbert Wu/Minden Pictures/FLPA; 17, © worldswildlifewonders/Shutterstock; 18, © blickwinkel/Alamy; 19T, © Hermann Eisenbeiss/Science Photo Library and © ptnphoto/Shutterstock; 19, © Hermann Eisenbeiss/Science Photo Library; 20T, chung toan co/Shutterstock; 20B, © Kenishirotie/Shutterstock; 21, © Peter Titmuss/Alamy; 22, © Ruby Tuesday Books; 23TL, © NatalieJean/Shutterstock; 23TC, © Hermann Eisenbeiss/Science Photo Library; 23TR, © Sever180/Shutterstock; 23BL, © Richard Whitcombe/Shutterstock; 23BC, © Ppaauullee/Shutterstock; 23BR, © Filipe B. Varela/Shutterstock.

Publisher: Kenn Goin
Senior Editor: Joyce Tavolacci
Creative Director: Spencer Brinker
Design: Emma Randall
Photo Researcher: Ruby Tuesday Books Ltd

Library of Congress Cataloging-in-Publication Data

Lawrence, Ellen, 1967– author.
Water plants : all wet! / by Ellen Lawrence.
pages cm. — (Plant-ology)
Summary: "In this book readers will learn about water plants"— Provided by publisher.
Audience: Ages 4–8.
Includes bibliographical references and index.
ISBN 978-1-62724-865-5 (library binding) — ISBN 1-62724-865-X (library binding)
— ISBN 978-1-64280-796-7 (pbk.)
1. Aquatic plants—Juvenile literature. 2. Water lilies—Juvenile literature. I. Title. II. Series: Lawrence, Ellen, 1967- Plant-ology.
QK916.L39 2016
581.7'6—dc23

2015015378

For more information, write to Bearport Publishing, 5357 Penn Avenue South, Minneapolis MN 55419.
Printed in the United States of America.

Contents

Lily Pads

It's a warm summer day.

Round, green lily pads float on the surface of a pond.

A frog sits on one of the pads, waiting to catch an insect.

So what exactly are these green floating pads?

They are the leaves of water lilies.

Water lilies are plants that live and grow in water.

Plants that grow in ponds, lakes, rivers, and oceans are known as aquatic plants.

Plant Parts

There are many different kinds of aquatic plants.

Some water plants have leaves, stems, flowers, and **roots**—just like plants that grow on land.

The roots take in water and **nutrients** from the muddy soil at the bottom of ponds, lakes, and rivers.

Attached to the roots are long stems.

At the end of each stem is a leaf or flower that floats on top of the water.

Unlike the stiff stems of most land-growing plants, the stems of water lilies are soft and floppy. Why do you think this is?

(See answer on page 24.)

Skunk cabbage is a water plant that grows in wet soil at the edges of ponds and lakes. It gets its name because it smells like a skunk!

Floating Plants

Other water plants float on ponds with their roots dangling below the water's surface.

The roots take in water and nutrients directly from the pond.

Water cabbages grow in this way.

Some plants, such as hornworts, float beneath the water and have no roots.

These plants take in water and nutrients through their leaves.

Many water plants, including water lilies and hornworts, are supported, or held up, by the water. If they are lifted out of water, these plants will flop over.

Tiny and Giant!

Water plants come in many shapes and sizes.

Duckweed is a tiny, round plant that floats on ponds.

Its flowers and roots are so small they can only be seen with a magnifying glass.

The giant water lily, however, is truly enormous.

Its huge, round, floating leaves can grow to more than 8 feet (2.4 m) across!

The bottom of a giant water lily leaf has special parts called ribs that keep it from sinking. Air gets trapped between the ribs and helps the leaf float.

On the Seashore

Some water plants, such as mangrove trees, grow in salty ocean water along seashores.

A mangrove tree has many roots that spread downward from its trunk and branches.

The strong roots keep the tree upright and hold it firmly in the ground.

This stops the tree from falling over when waves crash against it.

Look at the mangrove trees in this picture. If you could rename the trees, what would you call them? Try to think of a name that describes how they look or where they live.

Crocodiles, fish, and crabs live among the underwater roots of mangrove trees. Birds, monkeys, and insects make their homes in the trees' leafy branches.

An Underwater Meadow

Sea grass is a water plant that grows in oceans near the shore.

It has long, thin leaves that look like grasses that grow on land.

Sea grass grows in shallow water in huge underwater grasslands, or **meadows**.

Fish and other animals use these meadows to hide from their enemies.

Many sea animals also raise their babies in them.

Large plant-eating animals called manatees feed on sea grass.

sea grass meadow
stingray

What Is Seaweed?

Oceans are home to other living things that look like plants but are not, such as seaweed.

Seaweed is a type of living thing called **algae**.

Some seaweeds grow on the ocean floor or on underwater rocks.

Others float freely in the water.

One kind of seaweed has tiny balloon-like parts called bladders.

These air-filled bladders help the seaweed float in the water.

Kelp is a large, brown seaweed that grows on the seabed. Sea otters sometimes wrap kelp around their bodies to hold them in one place as they sleep in the ocean.

Trapped!

There are some underwater plants that are dangerous—but only to tiny animals!

Bladderworts are **carnivorous** plants that grow in ponds and rivers.

These plants have tiny traps on their underwater stems.

When an animal touches a trap, it is sucked inside.

Then the plant releases liquids that turn the animal into a soupy mush.

The mush contains nutrients that the bladderwort needs to survive.

bladderwort plants

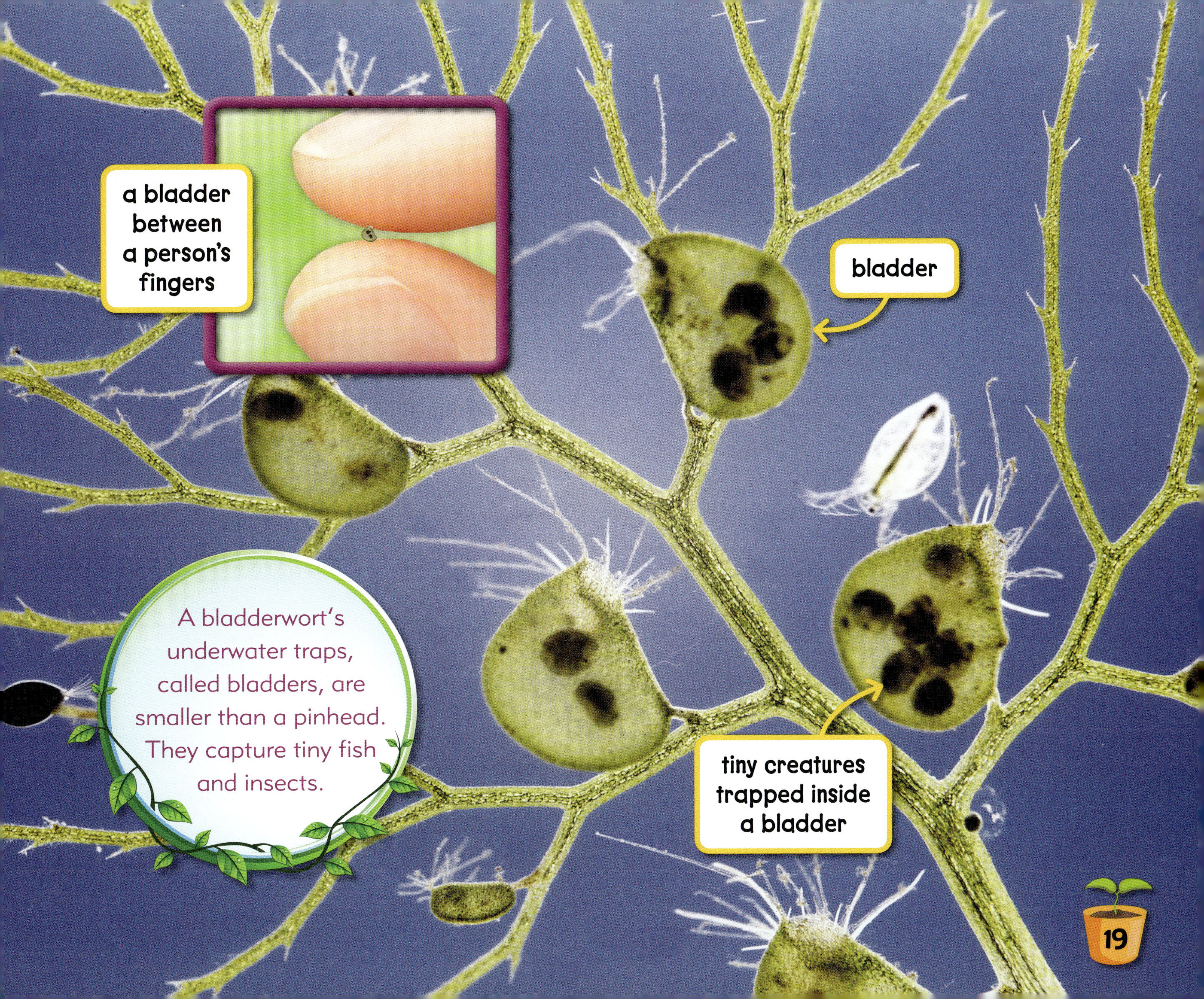

A bladderwort's underwater traps, called bladders, are smaller than a pinhead. They capture tiny fish and insects.

Water Plants to Eat

Some water plants, such as rice and water chestnuts, are grown by people for food.

Rice plants produce grains that people eat.

The bulb-like **corms** of water chestnuts are also used for food.

Water plants are useful and important to animals and people.

They make ponds, lakes, rivers, and oceans look beautiful, too!

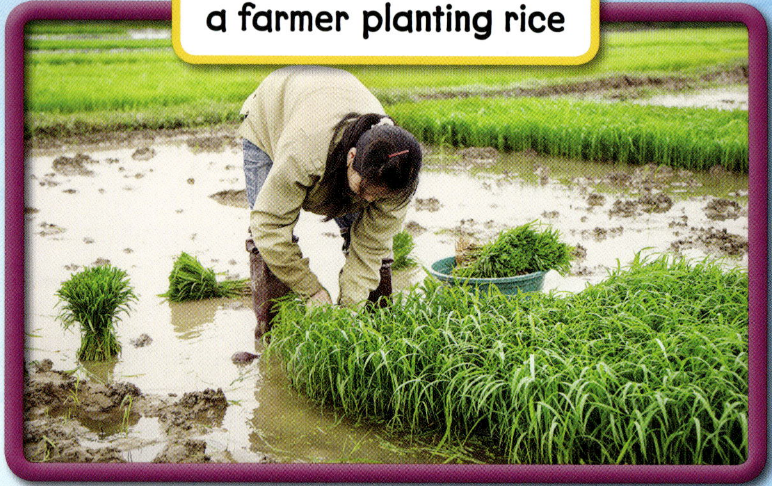

a farmer planting rice

water chestnut corms

Watercress is a leafy vegetable that has a peppery taste. Farmers grow this water plant in flooded fields.

farmers harvesting watercress

Science Lab

Make a model of lily pads

You will need:

- Gravel or small stones
- A large bowl
- Water
- Green string or yarn
- Scissors
- Duct tape
- Green plastic bottle caps

1. Place about 2 inches (5 cm) of gravel into a large bowl.
2. Slowly fill the bowl with water.
3. To make a lily pad and stem, cut a piece of string and tape it to the underside of a bottle cap. (The string must be slightly longer than the depth of the water in the bowl). Repeat this step with the other bottle caps.

4. Gently place one of the bottle caps on the surface of the water so that it floats. Then carefully tuck its string, or stem, under the stones—as if it were growing in a pond.
5. Repeat this step with the other bottle caps.
6. Show your model to your friends, family, or teacher.

- **Explain how the plant grows in the soil at the bottom of a pond.**
- **Show how the stems are supported by water but are floppy when lifted out of water.**
- **Explain how the pads, or leaves, float on the water's surface.**

Science Words

algae (AL-jee) plantlike living things, such as seaweed, that are often found in ponds, lakes, rivers, and oceans

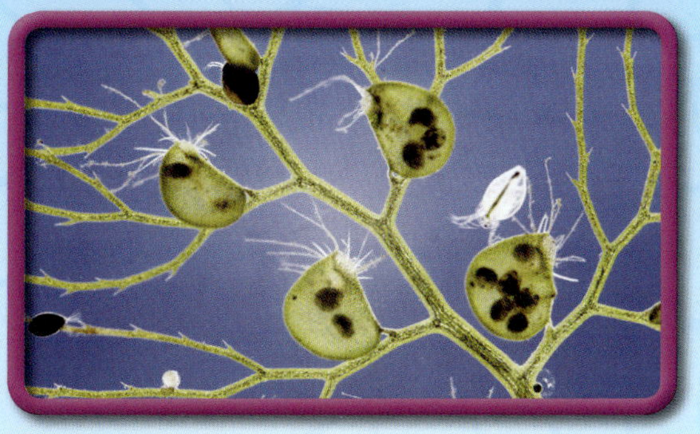

carnivorous (kar-NIV-ur-uhss) meat-eating; carnivorous plants catch insects and other small animals to obtain nutrients

corms (KAWRMS) large, underground parts of plant stems

meadows (MED-ohz) fields or underwater areas covered with grasses and other plants

nutrients (NOO-tree-uhnts) vitamins, minerals, and other substances needed by living things to grow and be healthy

roots (ROOTS) underground plant parts that take in water and nutrients from the soil

Index

Read More

King, Zelda. *Examining Pond Habitats (Graphic Organizers: Habitats)*. New York: PowerKids Press (2009).

Lindeen, Carol K. *Life in a Pond (Living in a Biome)*. North Mankato, MN: Capstone (2004).

Rissman, Rebecca. *Living and Nonliving in the Ocean (Is It Living or Nonliving?)*. Chicago: Raintree (2013).

Learn More Online

To learn more about about water plants, visit
www.bearportpublishing.com/Plant-ology

About the Author

Ellen Lawrence lives in the United Kingdom. Her favorite books to write are those about nature and animals. In fact, the first book Ellen bought for herself, when she was six years old, was the story of a gorilla named Patty Cake that was born in New York's Central Park Zoo.

Answer for Page 6

A water lily's stems are held up, or supported, by the water. Unlike land plants, the stems of aquatic plants don't need to be stiff to hold up leaves and flowers.